I can do all things

Written and illustrated by
SABRINA ADEWUMI

Thank you for purchasing an authorized copy of this book and for complying with copyright laws by not reproducing in any form without permission.
Copyright © 2023 All Rights Reserved

Scripture quotations marked NCV are taken from the New Century Version®. Copyright © 2005 by Thomas Nelson. Used by permission. All rights reserved.

For our three little birds,

and children everywhere whose faith in God means they

are destined for greatness.

I can climb the **highest mountains**

With God at my side
and faith in my heart

Nothing is impossible for me!

MARK 9:23

I may not be the

STRONGES~~T~~

the **TALLEST**

or the **BRAVEST**

But the Holy Spirit gives me

strength

My heart is filled with

COURAGE

to try things I've never done before

Like a lion, hear me...

PROVERBS 28:1

I don't need to be afraid or shy

when I am asked to speak

God gives me the

CONFIDENCE

I need

and strengthens me when I am weak

ISAIAH 40:29

If I don't have expensive clothes,

fancy gadgets

or the latest toy...

I still have **everything** I need.

In His presence there is fullness of

JOY!

PSALM 16:11

So no matter what path my life takes,
or what my circumstances may be

I know my future is secure -

    He's guiding me carefully

PSALM 37:23

And

whatever

I set my mind to do...

Through Christ who strengthens me!

PHILIPPIANS 4:13

I can do all things through Christ, because He gives me strength.

PHILIPPIANS 4:13 (NCV)

www.ingramcontent.com/pod-product-compliance
Lightning Source LLC
Chambersburg PA
CBHW051402110526
44592CB00023B/2924